The Healing Power of
a Father's Blessing

*Prayer of a loving Father
based on Psalm 23*

Linda Schubert
author of the best-selling
Miracle Hour

Foreword by Charles Whitehead

Nihil obstat: Kevin P. Joyce, Ph. D., *Censor deputatus*

Imprimatur: +Pierre DuMaine, Bishop of San Jose,
February 16, 1995

Other books by Linda Schubert

Miracle Hour
Five Minute Miracles

Coauthored with Rev. Robert DeGrandis, S.S.J.

Come, Follow Me
The Gift of Miracles
Resting in the Spirit
Renewed by the Holy Spirit
Praying for Miracles
Coming to Life
Healing Through the Mass
Healing the Broken Heart
Intergenerational Healing

Cover photo by Michael Powers
Half Moon Bay, California

Scripture quotations from New International Version
unless otherwise noted

Linda Schubert
Miracles of the Heart Ministries
P.O. Box 4034
Santa Clara, CA 95056
phone/fax (408) 734-8663

♥

"...I kneel before the Father, from whom His whole family in heaven and on earth derive its name. I pray that out of His glorious riches He may strengthen you with power through His Spirit in your inner being, so that Christ may dwell in your hearts through faith. And I pray that you, being rooted and established in love, may have power, together with all the saints, to grasp how wide and long and high and deep is the love of Christ, and to know this love that surpasses knowledge — that you may be filled to the measure of all the fullness of God" (Eph 3:14-19).

Contents

Foreword

A few weeks ago, when Sue and I were at a meeting with Linda Schubert, she asked us to pronounce a blessing on all the married people present. Then she asked me to give a father's blessing, and Sue a mother's, while others were invited to bless the single people. As we pronounced the blessings we realized they were having a noticeable impact. In Linda's words — blessings have powerful implications. After that day I found myself thinking a lot about blessings, and eagerly awaiting the book Linda told us she was writing. When the manuscript arrived, I stopped what I was doing and sat down to read it.

There are some books that immediately strike me as important. They seem to be published at exactly the right moment, and as I read them I get excited! I suppose I shouldn't really be surprised when this happens — after all, God is much more aware of our needs than we are and He's always guiding us one way or another. I think many of us will hear His voice as we read *The Healing Power of a Father's Blessing*. It's one of those inspired and timely books.

It's an important book because it brings to our attention something we have either forgotten or perhaps never even noticed — that words of blessing spoken over us can be life-changing. It's timely because we're living in an age of rapid and dramatic change, where everything is questioned and challenged. This means we can no longer take comfort in the traditional values of our society and the old ways of doing things. But we should take comfort in the knowledge that no matter what may be happening around us, we're sons and daughters of the Father and we're of enormous value in ourselves. And that's not all — we're also lovable and acceptable. What better way can we experience this than by blessing one another?

It's not only an important and timely book — it's also practical. Linda reminds us that blessings can be from God to men, and from men to men. They can be given by our Heavenly Father, and by our human fathers or by someone standing in for them. We would all do well to grasp this message eagerly, and to put it into practice. Then we would not only pronounce life-giving messages over one another — we would also be blessings to one another.

May the Lord bless and renew you as you read this book.

Charles Whitehead
London, England
President, International Catholic
Charismatic Renewal Services

I

Our Vision of the Blessing

Introduction

"...You, O Lord, are our Father..." (Is 63:16).

In my travels around the world conducting days of prayer and healing, each time I introduce the subject of "blessing" a stillness settles over people, as if fond memories or deep yearnings are stirred. A few times in healing services I have asked people to stand up if they have never received a father's blessing, or if they felt the blessing was somehow inadequate. Then I invite a mature "father" of the local community to stand before God in the "blessing gap," to extend a father's blessing in all the areas where they may have experienced this lack. From the reports I have received, it is a very healing experience for them. I'm continually amazed at how hungry people are for blessing and what a difference blessing makes in their lives. Seeing their craving and getting in touch with my own longing for blessing, especially from a father, has motivated me to write this book.

Perhaps the subject brings to you similar feelings. You may want to receive a father's blessing, even if you don't really understand what blessing is all about. The following prayer might be a starting point:

"God, I really don't understand the meaning of a father's blessing, but I want to understand. Scripture refers to You as God the Father, yet I don't know what it means for You to
be my Father. My experience of a loving father
is limited. I need Your love. I need a father. I
need blessing. I believe You are the one who can
give this blessing to me, but I don't understand
how to receive it. In spite of my uncertainties, I
am going to open my heart and receive this gift
from You. Thank You, Lord. Amen."

What is a blessing?

Some of the definitions of blessing include "approval;
encouragement; a thing conducive to happiness or welfare."
Other words associated with blessing include "benediction,
praise, honor, consecration, favor, good fortune, pardon."
The word "Eulogy" is associated with blessing in *Vine's Ex-
pository Dictionary,* and means "to speak well of, to speak
approvingly of." To bless a person is to say, "I see God's
goodness in you." To bless a person is to speak truth: God's
goodness is in them; you see it and say it. You encourage
them to see it too. Then...something wonderful happens.

A scripture that comes to mind is Ezekiel in the valley
of the dry bones. *"...Prophesy to these bones and say to them,
'Dry bones, hear the word of the Lord.' I (the Lord) will
make breath enter you, and you will come to life"* (Eze 37:4).
Blessings can speak to our "dry bones" and invite them to
come to life. We all need uplifting and encouragement.

Think of a blessing as the tender, healing voice of your
Heavenly Father (who often uses human voices to express
His intentions). He speaks unconditional love and acceptance into your blood and bones and sinews and tendons;
into heart, mind and soul. Consider it a prophetic love word

spoken deeply into your spirit, bringing dry and empty places to life. He invites us to believe Him when He says in Eze 37:14, *"...I the Lord have spoken, and I have done it...."* Jer 29:11 says, *"For I know the plans I have for you...plans to prosper you...plans to give you hope and a future."*

The Lord encourages us to believe that a word spoken in His name really means something and does something. *"As the rain and the snow come down from heaven, and do not return to it without watering the earth and making it bud and flourish, so that it yields seed for the sower and bread for the eater, so is My word that goes forth from My mouth: It will not return to Me empty, but will accomplish what I desire and achieve the purpose for which I sent it"* (Is 55:10-11). Something real and life-giving is transmitted through simple words of blessing.

Why focus on "FATHER" blessing?

All blessings have value, yet the father's blessing seems especially important, particularly in the present age when there is a need to strengthen and encourage fathers. A newspaper article reported that 37% of the children in the United States live apart from their fathers. In fact, fatherlessness is considered one of the most urgent social problems in the world today. Experts agree that much of our breakdown in society--the lawlessness, pornography, domestic violence, teenage pregnancy, abortion, school dropouts--is connected to fatherlessness. A television news program touched on this issue in discussing the lawless behavior of many of today's children. They spoke of how children need fathers to show them how adult males live. They reported how today's children have no restraining sense of how to behave. Some Christian leaders feel that the "father-wound" is one of the deepest wounds on earth. The lack of healthy bonding with fathers probably increases young people's vulnerability to anyone coming along offering love and friendship. This lack of protection makes them easy prey for cults and over-controlling religious groups.

Sometimes there is fatherlessness even with a live-in father, because he is emotionally absent, or doesn't provide a safe environment where children feel secure and free to grow. As one father said, remembering his alcoholic father, "I never had a father who took care of me." He has struggled to be a loving father without a good model. Even the best father, in the healthiest Christian home, isn't perfect. As one Christian counselor said, "Few young people these days come from a graced household."

Because of my lack of healthy bonding with my father, for many years I was extremely vulnerable to being dominated by people who would tell me what to do and what to think. I came to a point where I believed I couldn't think for myself. I kept trying to be what I was not, just to please people and to be accepted. Then I deeply encountered Jesus, and discovered that I had the right to be my own unique self. There was no more room in my life for the old bondage. Jesus comes to set us free with His liberating love.

Richard, father of eight and grandfather of nine, said to me, "I wasn't a bad father. I just wasn't a good loving father because I didn't know how." Many of today's fathers didn't have loving fathers who shared their lives with their children. They continue the pattern, and end up carrying guilt for not doing and being all their children need.

Release from guilt

We were created with a place in our hearts that only God the Father can fill. No matter how well a father tries to father, his children will still need a Father blessing from the Father of Jesus. That's why Jesus came--to take us to His Father. No matter how good or bad a natural father we had,

4

there is a deep cry in our hearts for a Father that can only be filled by Father God.

Whatever our relationship or lack of relationship with fathers; whatever blessing our fathers were able or unable to express, God has expressed His Fatherly purpose and blessing for us. *"'I will be a Father to you and you will be My sons and daughters,' says the Lord Almighty"* (2 Co 6:18).

When Richard began to get in touch with his feelings about father blessing, he prayed something like this:

"Lord, I give You my hurts, anger and pain connected with my earthly father. I'm sorry for any way I have learned to curse instead of bless. Let the family pattern change now from cursing to blessing. Let my lack and my hunger open me both to receive and give blessings."

With this prayer, Richard began a process of restoration. Through speaking and receiving God's words we too can begin a process of restoration.

Fathers who become aware of father-wounds in themselves and in their children need to know that pronouncing the blessing NOW can make a difference in their children's lives. It also relieves them of the guilt for not being the parents they wish they had been. Receiving the Father Blessing can make a difference in your own life and in the lives of your children and their children.

Reversing negative words

"...(He) turned the curse into a blessing for you, because the Lord your God loves you" (Dt 23:5).

We have all spoken negative words and been the target of words that wound. We have seen their destructive power.

For example: "You'll never be any good," "You're too dumb to learn," etc. (Most people have a lengthy list.) Let's take a moment and ask the Lord to release us from memories of negative words, spoken by us or to us.

Pray:

"Father, thank You for making me a new creation. I now receive Your Holy Spirit to enable me to speak Your Word to separate light from darkness. I say, 'Let there be light. Let the cleansing waters of Your Word wash away the debris of negative, unkind, defeating words I have accumulated, believed, and allowed to become a part of me. Shower me with the freshness of Your mercy and grace. Forgive me for the harmful words I've used toward others, spoken or unspoken. Please replace the hurt with Your healing blessing. Thank You, Father, that You want to do this. I now thank You and receive Your word of love and blessing, in Jesus' name. Amen.' "

Blessings in scripture

There are countless references to blessing in the Old and New Testament. In Ge 1:28 God created Adam and Eve and then blessed them: *"...God blessed them, and said to them, 'Be fruitful and increase in number....'* He blessed Abraham and his descendants in Ge 22:17-18: *"...because you have not withheld your son, your only son, I will surely **bless** you and make your descendants numerous as the stars in the sky...and through your offspring all nations on earth will be blessed...."*

Jacob pronounced blessings on his sons. His blessing of his son Joseph is recorded in Ge 49:23-26 (NAB): *"By the*

6

*power of the Mighty One of Jacob, because of the Shepherd, the Rock of Israel, the God of your father, who helps you, God Almighty, who **blesses** you, with the blessings of the heavens above, the blessings of the abyss that crouches below, the blessing of breasts and womb, the blessings of fresh grain and blossoms, the blessings of the everlasting mountains, the delights of the eternal hills. May they rest on the head of Joseph, on the brow of the prince among his brothers."*

Moses pronounced blessings on the tribes of Israel in Dt 33. His blessing of Asher is recorded in verses 24-27: *"Most blessed of sons is Asher; let him be favored by his brothers, and let him bathe his feet in oil. The bolts of your gates will be iron and bronze, and your strength will equal your days. There is no one like the God of Jeshurun, who rides on the heavens to help you and on the clouds in His majesty. The eternal God is your refuge, and underneath are the everlasting arms. He will drive out your enemy before you...."*

Scripture points to the duty of the priests to bless the people in the name of the Lord, referred to as a benediction. In Nu 6:23-26 (NAB) the Lord said to Moses: *"Speak to Aaron and his sons and tell them: This is how you shall bless the Israelites.*

> *'The Lord bless you and keep you!*
> *The Lord let His face shine upon you*
> *and be gracious to you!*
> *The Lord look upon you kindly*
> *and give you peace!'*

> *Then the Lord said, 'So shall they invoke My name upon the Israelites, and I will bless them'"* (Nu 6:27).

Jesus blessed the little children in Mk 10:16: *"And He took the children in His arms, put His hands on them and blessed them."* Through word and touch He made a deep life-changing connection with them. The topic of blessing is clearly important to God.

Experiences of blessing

"...The blessing of the Lord be upon you; we bless you in the name of the Lord" (Ps 129:8).

Nancy, a friend for many years, has a regular habit of saying "God bless you" to people she meets along the way. In the car I've heard her say, "God bless you" to inconsiderate drivers. It's an automatic response of love. She also enjoys saying "Bless your heart" to people, even strangers who cross her path. Frequently they will respond gratefully, "Oh, thank you! I need my heart blessed today." Something in them seems to blossom when she conveys this simple blessing. *"My purpose is that they may be encouraged in heart..."* (Col 2:2).

At age 2-1/2, Jason knew the power of blessing. During a Sunday morning church service when his mother and grandmother, Kay and Barbara, were about to walk up the aisle to receive communion, Jason suddenly took off at a run, racing up the aisle ahead of them with hands folded in prayer. "My blessing, my blessing," he yelled to his embarrassed mother.

I know a couple with ten children who grew up with a tradition of daily blessings. Every morning the father or mother would stand at the door as the children left for school, make the sign of the cross on each forehead and ask God's blessing and protection. It seemed to be a moment of value for each of them.

Another family practices "forgiveness-blessing." When tension and conflict disrupts their unity they gather in a circle in the living room with a chair in the middle. One at a time they sit in the chair and ask forgiveness for offenses committed. The seven-year-old son might say to his sister, "I'm sorry I broke your toy. Please forgive me." Then the family members extend forgiveness and affirm the one in the chair. They close with a blessing and prayer. Then someone else sits in the chair. Sometimes when there is tension in the family, the children remind the parents, "It's time for the forgiveness thing" again. Forgiveness, given and received, is a powerful avenue of blessing.

A friend, Madeleine, was raised in Malta by parents who communicated to their children the importance of blessing. The first thing the children did in the morning was to go to one parent then the other and say, "Good morning, Mummy. Bless me. Good morning, Daddy. Bless me." Each parent responded, "Good morning, darling, God bless you." Madeleine and her brother and sisters never left the house without asking for and receiving their parents' blessing. As adults, they have passed the tradition on to their children.

Jason's grandmother, Barbara, recalls how her father prayed with her as a schoolgirl, nightly asking God's blessing on her life. As a woman in her late fifties, she shared about the power of his blessing. Living in her father's approval, she grew up with courage to go out and explore, travel, and try new things. His blessing released life into her; it was in a sense an enabling grace that moved her forward. She didn't have to go out and search for a blessing, or struggle to prove her worth, as so many people do. She knew deep in her soul that she was loved and supported. She greatly appreciates the benefit of her father's blessing in her life. *"A father's blessing gives a family firm roots..."* (Sir 3:9 NAB).

Then too, there is sometimes a sense of blessing, a lovely healing work sovereignly accomplished by God that can only be described as a blessing. Consider the following example:

Little girl dressed in shame

"Little girl, I say to you, arise" (Mk 5:41 NAB).

I was in my mid-forties when this healing event occurred. During prayer one day I saw in an interior vision a girl of about eight years old crouched under a kitchen table in a dirty white dress. Jesus came to her, reached out and took her hand, and drew her to her feet, saying with tenderness and compassion, "Little girl dressed in shame." As He touched her hand and spoke the words, she became radiant, and her clothing changed to a yellow dotted swiss party dress. They twirled around the kitchen together in a joyful dance. I was that little girl, and knew the Lord was healing a deep scar related to my father.

A couple of reflections seem important here. First, Jesus spoke the truth of how I felt (dressed in shame). The words were like a laser beam pinpointing something in the past that caused me to hide and turn inward and feel dirty. He spoke the truth of how I felt then took me beyond, to the greater truth of who I am in Him. His freeing me from this shameful memory is one of the beautiful ways my Heavenly Father re-parented me. Jesus comes to heal, to bless, to set us free. *"You turned my wailing into dancing; you removed my sackcloth and clothed me with joy"* (Ps 30:11).

My experience with Dad

I was one who yearned for a father's blessing. When I was in my thirties I asked Dad one time if he would pray and ask Jesus to take away my headache. We were alone in the car, it was evening and the headache had bothered me all afternoon. This was the first time I had ever asked my father to pray for me. He was an atheist, an emotionally absent father, whose touch was not always healing. I never felt safe in his arms. I can't remember ever going to him with a serious problem, or asking his advice, or receiving counsel for any of the big issues of life. He never knew that I had breast cancer; I never told him I had a mastectomy. I didn't want to discuss something as personal as my breasts with him. I needed fatherly love concerning this life-threatening disease, and I was afraid it wouldn't be fatherly. I grew into middle age without sharing the highs and lows of life with him.

But this one time I did request that he put his hand on my head and ask Jesus to take away my headache. He hesitantly placed his rough, carpenter's hand on my head and said, "Jesus, take away my headache." He didn't even say the words right, but my headache left. By acting on the inspiration to honor him I released the power of God's word in the commandment, "Honor your father and mother." Ephesians 6:2-3 says, *"Honor your father and mother...that it may go well with you...."*

Actually, there was one deep, profound moment of communication between Dad and me. He was 85 years old, then a Christian, and he was dying. I sat beside him on his deathbed as he lay in a coma. The only sound he made was the rattling in his throat that signaled death was near. For many years I had prayed for healing in my relationship with him. In my life I had a pattern of running away from men, and knew this was partly connected to not feeling safe in Daddy's arms. So I sat with my hand on his chest, praying quietly for a long time, stirred by old memories. After a while I sensed the presence of the Lord in a special way, and something changed. Then my father spoke two words that shot out like bullets from a high powered rifle, yet another person in the room would not have heard a whisper. He said, "I'm sorrrrrryyyyy!" Those words traveled some forty years back to touch a little girl's wounded spirit, and something came to rest inside. I said, "I forgive you, Daddy." The next day he died. In the months and years to come I discovered a new freedom to enjoy the friendship of men, and less need to run away at the first sign of trouble in a relationship. His "I'm sorry" touched my heart like a benediction. It too, had the quality of a blessing. My capacity to trust God as loving Father increased through that healing experience.

A European woman's experience

"He satisfies my desires with good things..."
(Ps 103:5).

Once after sharing this story during a meeting in Canada, a European woman told me a similar story about her father. She was sitting with him and going through a forgiveness process as he lay unconscious, near death. She spoke with the vulnerability of a child: "Daddy, I need your blessing before you die. Please give me your blessing." He responded, spirit to spirit, as my dad had spoken to me: "I give you my blessing. I bless you." He died soon after the words were spoken. There was a settling in her spirit, a sense of resolution and a new courage to move on with her life. In his final moments he gave her something she had longed to receive all her life. His blessing nourished a place in her heart that had been dry and empty. She, too, acknowledged the place of her father in her heart, a decision that enabled God's word to work.

In His time

"He has made everything beautiful in its time..." (Ecc 3:11).

Several years after my father died, I was on an airplane flying from San Francisco to New Orleans when I saw a bright and shining vision of my father's face. As I gazed at

12

it in wonderment I heard the voice of the Lord saying in my heart, "Now, receive into yourself the goodness of your father."

Because of hurts of the past, I had shut myself off from the good as well as the not so good. In doing this, I had lost a certain vitality in my life that could have come from my father. So I simply said, "Yes, Lord, I receive *from you* the goodness of my father." In that moment I felt new courage, strength and vitality come into my life. I began to remember the good things: his kindness, his creativity, his honorable nature as a businessman. I remembered the time he tried to save a little girl who had fallen down a waterfall. I was able then to begin thanking the Lord for the gift of my father.

On another occasion I was driving past a house where I had lived as a child. As fear and sadness began to rise in me, I again heard the voice of the Lord in my heart. His voice was rich with compassion as He poured these words through my heart: "Your father didn't know how to love and he didn't know how to do things right. He just didn't know how." Later, as I reflected on the Lord's word, I realized something important: I couldn't have heard those words if I had not already decided to unconditionally love Dad and decided to fulfill the commandment to honor him. Jesus lives in us to fulfill the purposes of God in us.

During the encounter with the Lord on my drive that day, I felt some of His feelings for my dad. Wanting to make a response, I said out loud as I drove, **"Jesus, I want to be healed. Help me to learn to allow Your healing in my life."** I have discovered in many situations it is necessary to express these kinds of thoughts out loud to Jesus. Getting the words out seems to make a wider opening for the healing process.

My prayer for you, is that you will be open to this kind of healing. I pray you will bring to Jesus any negative, pain-

13

ful feelings, speak the truth and hear from Him the truth; then allow Him to bring you into the truth of who you are in Him. I pray you will enter into the wholeness and uniqueness that is your gift from your Heavenly Father. I pray that in the right time you will see your earthly father through the eyes of your Heavenly Father. And I pray in the Lord's time you will be able to receive into yourself the goodness of your father.

Learning about a God of love

I pray for you that Jesus will bring to mind certain instances which, while they were not specific blessings, had the quality of blessing. Perhaps it was the kindness of a police officer, a fatherly act by a neighbor, a healing word from a teacher--someone who showed you what a father could be like. While God is bigger and better, it was still a glimpse of a father. My prayer is that you will come to see blessings in events of the past that at the time you didn't or couldn't recognize as a blessing. And I pray He will give many father-figures, to spiritually father you along the way.

God doesn't leave us orphans. He says in Ps 27:10, *"Though my father and mother forsake me, the Lord will receive me."* I'm reminded of a favorite African proverb: "God makes a way through no way." Jesus will take us to the Father, who will always receive us and never forsake us. He will often use someone else's earthly father to bring the experience of father-blessing to us.

The Holy Spirit enables other people's fathers to model Christ for us (to teach us who we are in Christ). Through them we can learn about a God of love; a God we can trust; a God who is dependable and trustworthy. They can introduce us to a spirituality that frees our hearts and minds to reach out and grow. With this as a foundation, we can make the transition to trusting our loving Heavenly Father.

14

A friend, Don, told me about a time in his life when he was going through a powerful spiritual awakening. His father, a businessman and non-practicing Catholic, didn't understand his nature and didn't have the capacity to nurture his son's spiritual development. The Lord provided Ernie to spiritually re-parent him. Don said, "I don't know what would have happened if Ernie hadn't been there, listening, affirming, and providing a guiding father principle." His fatherly presence and warm, healthy spirituality provided a nurturing environment in which Don could feel free to grow. At a critical time in Don's life, Ernie let him see inside his own spiritual process, without trying to control or direct. Don said, "He brought healing and openness to my spirit." Today, Don is a spiritual father for many young men and women.

Stand-in blessings from a "father" of the community

> *"I looked for a man among them who would build up the wall and stand before me in the gap..."* (Eze 22:30).

In healing services when I ask people to stand up if they need a father's blessing, usually quite a few people stand up, while others admit later that in their hearts they "stood up," but didn't want anyone to know. Some fear if they admit the lack they would be dishonoring their father. (The truth sets us free to be healed.) I ask a father to pray the blessing because it's important to have the words pronounced in a male voice.

The stand-in father prays for them to know in their hearts that they were always loved and wanted. 1 Jn 4:16 (NAB) says, *"We have come to know and to believe in the love God has for us. God is love, and he who abides in love abides in God, and God in him."* Our calling as Christians is to love,

15

yet we can't love until the places within our hearts are filled with His love. We need to "know and believe."

The "father" who speaks the blessing asks God the Father to reach into their lives and pour His love into their spirits; to touch the child-heart that never knew love to the extent it was needed; to bless the unblessed areas of their souls. He prays that they will feel safe in God's love and let down their barriers; that they will trust Him with their lives. He prays that they will let go of chronic negative expectations and the need to fail. He prays they will let go of rebellion, the excessive need to prove themselves, and all destructive behavior. He prays that they will come into a deeper knowledge of being a loved person; that they will feel free and safe to grow emotionally and spiritually. He prays that they will experience healing of the name "father." He prays that every scar and sore in their soul associated with the name "father" will be replaced with a soft awareness that Jesus was there, loving them all the time. *"For you shall forget your misery; you shall remember it as waters that pass away"* (Jb 11:16).

He prays that our Heavenly Father will breathe His love deep into their hearts--that His love will touch emotions like grief and guilt and shame and anger and fear; that His love will touch and heal crippling memories of a father who was abusive, absent, incestuous, judgmental, critical, harsh, unloving and all the other negative experiences.

He prays for deep healing in their minds; for the courage to rise up and take responsibility for their lives; to move from victim to victor in Jesus. He prays for growth in trust and inner fortitude, for protection from harm, for freedom to enjoy life to the full. It's a powerful prayer with deep healing effects. *"...I have come that they may have life, and have it to the full"* (Jn 10:10).

16

Positive feedback

After a male representative of the community prayed a father's blessing at a conference where I was speaking, I received a letter from a jubilant participant. She said, "Because of the conference I started telling my family, 'God bless you.' They first mumbled something back, then said, 'You too.' Now they say 'God bless you.' This is progress for all of us!"

At that same conference there were three generations of one family present, including the 80-year-old father. After the blessing during the Saturday evening healing service, the five family members gathered in a private room at the request of one daughter, to receive their father's blessing. With their coaching, he stood before his family, raised his hand and pronounced a blessing on them. It was a unique event in the family, and deeply moving. In asking him for the blessing, they were honoring him and encouraging him to accept a vital position of spiritual leadership in the family. Other conference participants, when they learned of the father's family blessing, were also deeply touched. Some were moved to tears.

Benefits for the "father" praying the blessing

"...he who refreshes others will himself be refreshed" (Pr 11:25).

When we ask men at conferences to pray a father's blessing, we discover added benefits. The men communicating the blessing receive probably as much healing as the intended recipients. Through giving the blessing to others, men can gain a better understanding of their identity in Christ. They can also come into a deeper sense of their masculine heritage and have a clearer picture of their manhood, balancing courage with compassion; the strong leader with the tender lover, etc.

They can begin to assume a healthier fatherly role in their home, with their growing spiritual leadership building security and order into the family structure. They can find it easier to introduce their children to their Heavenly Father, and help them grow in that relationship. Through praying the Father Blessing for others, they can become aware of their powerful potential as a mentor to help boys and men grow into healthy fatherhood; and also be a model for girls and women who need to observe and experience godly fathers.

After reading a draft of this book, Richard felt empowered in three areas: First, it helped him feel the love of his Heavenly Father. Second, he was aware of now being able to claim the (implied) blessing his father gave before he died. Third, he felt finally ready to give his eight grown children his blessing. As an aside, Richard said Psalm 23, which is the format of our prayer, was a favorite scripture that "led him through troubled waters" at age 19 when his dad died.

Prayer for the pray-er

"...men spoke from God as they were carried along by the Holy Spirit" (2 Pe 1:21).

"Heavenly Father, we ask for a special anointing for the father-figure praying the blessing. Release Your love and healing power through his words. Let them accomplish Your purpose in the giver and receiver. Let the man pronouncing the blessing deeply believe the words he speaks. Loving Father, prepare him to be an open channel of Your healing grace. Give him Your words. Let the written prayers just be

18

a springboard to spontaneous blessings. If he needs healing in his fathering, allow that healing to begin as he prays for others. Thank You for the power of the Holy Spirit touching, healing and anointing him now in his inmost being. Let him speak from Your heart and be carried along by Your Holy Spirit to heal the deep father-wounds of the people. In Jesus' name we pray. Amen."

"My message and my preaching were not with wise and persuasive words, but with a demonstration of the Spirit's power, so that your faith might not rest on men's wisdom, but on God's power" (1 Cor 2:4-5).

II

Preparing to Receive the Blessing

A lesson from Bartimaeus and my mother

In the story of the blind beggar who received his sight, Jesus asked Bartimaeus, *"What do you want me to do for you?"* He responded from the depths of his heart, "Lord, I want to see" (Lk 18:41). Maybe that is what you want, also. Through the blessing you might want to see the goodness in people; to see your own goodness. You may want to see life through eyes of love, instead of eyes of fear. You might want to ask the Lord to show you the hidden blessings in your life.

At one low point in my mother's life, the Lord asked her a similar question. Dad had run away with another woman after more than 40 years of marriage, and Mom was confronted with what to do with her life. One day the Lord asked her, "Elizabeth, what do you REALLY WANT?" Her response, after deep searching, was, "Lord, I really want a marriage." He replied gently, "Loving Charlie is my choice for you, too." Then she laid her deep desires at the foot of the cross, entrusted into His care. In time my father returned and was converted, probably through her self-sacrificial love, her living out Gal 2:20: *"I have been crucified with Christ and I no longer live, but Christ lives in me...."* She learned that in her weakness she could step aside and allow the Lord's grace of forgiveness and blessing to flow to her husband. She learned, day by day, that she could trust the Lord to change her feelings. Elizabeth and Charlie celebrated more than 50 years of marriage before he died. At his funeral she said to the Lord, "Thank You for teaching me how to live Your love." Living His love is living a life of blessing.

What do YOU really want?

"Delight yourself in the Lord and He will give you the desires of your heart" (Ps 37:4).

As we prepare to pray the Father's Blessing, my question to you is this? What do you really want the Lord to do for you through this blessing? Sometimes we honestly don't know what we want, and we need to ask the Lord to show us what it is. Once when I was in Jerusalem I was wandering around the souvenir shops looking for something to buy, but nothing appealed to me. In a moment of frustration I turned to the Lord and said, "Please find something I really want." In a few moments I found myself in a little shop with ceramics and hand-blown glass. I was drawn to a piece of turquoise glass. Holding it almost reverently, I turned it over and looked at the little gold and black label which read, "Hebron glass." Hebron--an ancient town south of Jerusalem where the Old Testament patriarchs were buried--was the one place I had wanted to go, but couldn't.

As I held the turquoise glass, in some wonderful way that I can't begin to understand, the Lord took me to Hebron in my heart. Think about the desire of your heart; and if you don't really know what you want through the blessing, ask the Lord to show you.

A matter of trust

"Trust in the Lord with all your heart and lean not on your own understanding..." (Pr 3:5).

Jesus knows us intimately and wants us to know Him intimately. Intimacy requires trust. He wants us to trust Him. When we trust someone there is an assured reliance on the character, ability, and truth of someone. We have confidence in the person; we know the person is trustworthy; we depend on that person. Ps 125:1 says, *"Those who trust in the Lord are like Mt. Zion, which cannot be shaken but endures forever."* Then in Is 26:3 the Lord says, *"You will keep in perfect peace him whose mind is steadfast, because he trusts in You."*

The Father's Blessing is presented in the format of the 23rd Psalm, because it is a psalm of trust. Through this psalm the Lord wants us to be convinced that He loves us, and that we can trust in Him. He wants us to know He loves us just the way we are, no matter what we have done. He loved us before we were born and He loves us now. He will continue to love us no matter what we do. He knows that if we are certain we are loved by Him, we will be able to trust Him; when we can trust Him, we can entrust to Him our lives and everything else of value. We will begin to know, deep in our hearts, what it means that God is our Father.

I pray that no matter what your "father experience" has been until now, the Holy Spirit will plant deep in your heart a knowledge of God as loving Father who desires to liberate you into a life of deep satisfaction. The truth of His liberating love can only come by grace; and I pray that this grace comes to you now. I pray you will know that He loves you deeply, completely, unconditionally; and that you can trust Him with your life. Will you choose to believe this by faith? Understanding usually comes after we take the leap of faith.

Say: "I choose to believe with my heart that You are a loving Father; that You love me very much. I place my trust in You."

Receiving the blessing

"...what was sown on good soil is the man who hears the word and understands it. He produces a crop, yielding a hundred, sixty or thirty times what was sown" (Mt 13:23).

To "receive" a blessing is to reach out and gather it in; to take it; to harvest it; to welcome it; to give entrance to it. It's like taking a gift-wrapped package, opening it and saying, "Thank you." At one time (perhaps more than once) didn't you ask Jesus to come into your heart and be your Savior and Lord? You received Him, and continue to receive Him, and life has changed in a fundamental way. Think about how you received Him. We receive blessings from Him in much the same way. You might say: "I accept this gift; this blessing. I allow it into myself to heal me and change me."

Whether you receive the Father's Blessing alone in prayer, or through another person praying it for you, accept it from the heart of your loving Heavenly Father, whose power is greater than any power that holds you down; whose love is greater than your fear; whose resources are greater than your need. Receive it from your loving Father, through Jesus, by the action of the Holy Spirit who pours the love of God into our hearts. *"And hope does not disappoint us, because God has poured out His love into our hearts by the Holy Spirit, whom He has given us"* (Ro 5:5). Receive the blessing more than once, and at different levels.

Receive the blessing from a God who knows you intimately. Meditate on the words of Psalm 139: *"O Lord, You have searched me and You know me. You know when I sit and when I rise; You perceive my thoughts from afar. You discern my going out and my lying down; You are familiar with all my ways...You created my inmost being; You knit me together in my mother's womb. I praise You because I am fearfully and wonderfully made..."* (Ps 139:1-3, 13-14).

Just come to Jesus

"I am the way, the truth and the life. No one comes to the Father except through Me. If you really knew Me, you would know my Father as well... Anyone who has seen Me has seen the Father" (Jn 14:6-7, 9).

You might be saying, "But I'm not wonderfully made." "I'm broken, sick and ugly." "I've run away down wrong paths." "I've hurt people." "I'm angry." "I'm irresponsible." "Nobody likes me." You may have a litany of failures and excuses to present to the Lord but He will quiet your arguments and say, "No child of mine is ugly. I am a God of restoration, so come. Just come. Give it all to me. I am the answer to your need. Let Me forgive you. Let Me love you. I created you to love you."

He will remind you of Isaiah 53:4-5: *"Surely He took up our infirmities and carried our sorrows...He was pierced for our transgressions, He was crushed for our iniquities; the punishment that brought us peace was upon Him, and by His wounds we are healed."* God, through Jesus, redeemed us from sin, failure and ugliness. Jesus took upon Himself sin, failure and ugliness. He did it for us to present us to the Heavenly Father. God became man, making it possible for our potential to be realized, and for us to be loved into wholeness. All He wants is for us to say "Yes," and cooperate with His wonderful plan for our lives.

At the Jordan River, God the Father spoke these words during the baptism of Jesus: *"You are My Son, whom I love; with you I am well pleased"* (Lk 3:22). He says to you, "You are My child whom I love; with you I am well pleased." Receive this blessing now. Let the words enter your soul. Just open your heart and let them into those areas that have not yet received or responded to that kind of love.

He holds you and blesses you

"He tends His flock like a shepherd; He gathers the lambs in His arms and carries them close to His heart..." (Is 40:11).

Choose to believe that He is now standing before you with His hands on your head as a fatherly benediction. Or believe He is holding you in His arms, as a shepherd holds a baby lamb; or as the father holds the little child in the cover photograph. As He holds you close, He speaks a blessing into your life through the avenue of the 23rd Psalm, as spoken to you intimately and personally. In the warmth of His arms, tell Him now, "Lord, I receive."

III

A Father's Prayer for Blessing

> *"I keep asking that the God of our Lord Jesus Christ, the glorious Father, may give you the Spirit of wisdom and revelation, so that you may know Him better. I pray also that the eyes of your heart may be enlightened in order that you may know the hope to which He has called you, the riches of His glorious inheritance in the saints, and His incomparably great power for us who believe..."* (Eph 1:17-19).

Psalm 23 — The Lord is your Shepherd

> *"I am the Good Shepherd. The Good Shepherd lays down His life for His sheep"* (Jn 10:11).

Jesus, the Good Shepherd, gave His life for you in loving obedience to His Father. Your response to that love gives you the right to call God your Father. May you recognize your need of Him, and say from your heart, "Yes, I want You for my Savior and my Lord. I want You to be the Shepherd of my soul." May your voice join with generations of men, women and children through the ages who have said, "Jesus, I believe in You. I receive You as my Savior and Lord."

May you look at Jesus your Shepherd and see your Heavenly Father, the Chief Shepherd. May you come to know the wonderful Fatherhood of God through your growing friendship with Jesus. You can trust Him with your life. May you know that nothing can ever separate you from His love.

Jesus, the Poured out Love of the Father, gives you all the love you need for yourself and others. Filled with His love, may you desire to turn away from anything that separates you from Him. May you choose to be sorry for your sins, and tell Him so. May you know that being with Him is the most important thing in your life, and separation from Him leads you into darkness and sorrow. May you experience His forgiveness, and forgive yourself.

May Jesus, the Baptizer in the Holy Spirit, pour out His Spirit on you in abundance. May you know the love and the power of His Spirit as it flows through every aspect of your nature. May you yield to the movement of the Spirit in your life, and give Him freedom to do whatever He wants. May you _____.
(Ask the Lord to give you His words.)

Jesus, Beloved of the Father, gives His life to you. May His presence bring acceptance of rightness in your heart; a sense of approval; a secure feeling of belonging. May the Holy Spirit deep inside draw you closer to your Father, Abba, Daddy. May you relax in the arms of your Shepherd and trust in His love. May you come to know and believe and trust in the love of your Father.

❤

"For God so loved the world that He gave His one and only son, that whoever believes in Him shall not perish but have eternal life" (Jn 3:16).

"...God sent the Spirit of His Son into our hearts, the Spirit who calls out, 'Abba, Father.' So you are...a son; and since you are a son, God has made you also an heir" (Gal 4:6-7).

"...God exalted Him to the highest place and gave Him the Name that is above every name, that at the Name of Jesus every knee should bow in heaven and on earth, and every tongue confess that Jesus Christ is Lord to the glory of God the Father" (Php 2:9-11).

(2 Co 5:17, Col 1:12, 2 Co 9:15, Ro 8:39, Jn 10:14-15, Ro 10:12, 1 Jn 4:13, 2 Co 3:17, Heb 2:13, Ro 8:16, 1 Jn 1:3, Ps 2:7)

You shall not want

"My God will meet all your needs according to His glorious riches in Christ Jesus" (Php 4:19).

Jesus, the Treasure of our Father, knows and cares about your deepest needs. In Him, you shall not want. He is your resource in every challenge; your provision in every need. May you know Him as your answer to every question; your response to every situation. May you look to Jesus for everything you need in work, in play, in relationships, in every dimension of life. Jesus, the visible image of God your Father, is your wisdom in the confusion of life; your light in darkness; your integrity in temptation; your trust for provision; your daily bread. May you trust Him with your health, your finances, your family, your friendships, your future. May your

union with Him be so total that your automatic response to every challenge is the simple question, "Jesus, how do You want me to respond to this?" "How should I feel about that?" May the words, "Jesus, I trust in You," be your response to every need. May you _____.
(Ask the Lord for His words.)

May you experience His nature and character forming in you as you trust Him to meet everyday needs. May you know Him in every moment and rely on Him in every circumstance. May you always remember that you belong to Him; and it's His job to take care of you. May you come to know and believe and trust in the love of your Father.

♥

"...I am the Bread of Life. He who comes to Me will never go hungry, and he who believes in Me will never be thirsty" (Jn 6:35).

"May the God of peace...that great Shepherd of the Sheep, equip you with everything good for doing His will, and may He work in us what is pleasing to Him through Jesus Christ, to whom be glory for ever and ever" (Heb 13:20-21).

"And God is able to make all grace abound to you, so that in all things at all times, having all you need, you will abound in every good work" (2 Co 9:8).

(Ps 147:14, Is 40:31, Mt 14:20, Mt 6:26, Lk 12:12, Php 4:13, Mt 6:32, 1 Co 2:9, Mt 7:7-11)

He makes you to lie down in green pastures

"The Lord your God is with you, He is mighty to save. He will take great delight in you, He will

29

quiet you with His love, He will rejoice over you with singing" (Zep 3:17).

Jesus, who reveals the tenderness of the Father, is loving you right now. May you hear His love words in your soul, and feel Him rocking you in Daddy's arms. He's bringing to life the little child in you. The heart of Jesus, pumping His precious blood through your veins, is giving you a life transfusion. Let it happen. Let it come. May the transfusion wash away the trash and debris of your life; all that troubles you; all the broken fragments of your life; all disturbance, turmoil and confusion. May His precious blood flowing in your veins, bring confidence in God's ability to control the chaos. In Him there is balance and order.

Jesus, your Hiding Place, offers you an alternative to being strong and independent. May you know that your dependence on Him is a sign of maturity, not weakness. May you open to Him like a trusting child, admitting your need, knowing you don't have to perform or be strong or be right. You just need to be His.

May you relax and accept His life in you. May you be comfortable in His love and His way of doing things. May you be comfortable with yourself, just the way you are. In the deep quiet of His heart may you come to accept yourself at the core of your being.

May you linger in the center of His heart, listening to the symphony of His love. May your heart settle into the rhythm of His own. Even now He Fathers you, nurtures you and pours His life into you. May you relax and enjoy His warm parental affection. May you _____.

The Lord, who is the peace of our Father,

30

blesses you with a deep refreshing peace as you commune with Him in the fresh green pastures of His love. May you remember with gratitude, that your life belongs to God. May you come to know and believe and trust in the love of your Father.

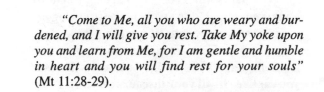

"Come to Me, all you who are weary and burdened, and I will give you rest. Take My yoke upon you and learn from Me, for I am gentle and humble in heart and you will find rest for your souls" (Mt 11:28-29).

"The Lord gives strength to His people; the Lord blesses His people with peace" (Ps 29:11).

" '...Not by might nor by power, but by My Spirit,' says the Lord" (Zec 4:6).

(Pr 3:24, 2 Ch 20:12, Jn 14:27, Jer 10:23, 2 Co 6:18, Ps 89:27, Ps 62:1, Ps 91:1)

He leads you beside quiet waters

"I will instruct you and teach you in the way you should go; I will counsel you and watch over you" (Ps 32:8).

Jesus, Beloved Teacher sent from the Father, is the wisdom for your life. He walks with you and talks with you and invites you on a fruitful journey. Jesus, who respects your free will, journeys with you as a trusted friend. May you listen attentively to Him and talk to Him openly and freely about the things that concern you. Jesus, our Wonderful Counselor, helps you see your life more clearly--where you are now, and where you are going. He helps you process your thoughts and feelings. He helps you to know yourself. May you trust Him with all the secret places of your heart. May you know that your unique nature is important to Jesus. May you know your responsibility to God to cooperate with the Holy Spirit in bringing about God's plan for your life.

May Jesus, the Living Word, help you to see and reverse any hidden vows never to love again; never to trust; never to let anyone get too close. May you give Him permission to uncover buried feelings and bring to light memories that hold you captive. In all your discouragements, weaknesses and failures may you say, "Jesus, I place my trust in You." May He bless you with a teachable spirit.

May you trust Him with your anger and frustration and all your emotions. May you trust Him to heal your emotional life as you hold your heart open to Him. May you learn how to express feelings in healthy ways. May you_____
_____.

Jesus, who loves you and cares about all your needs, brings insight into your inner workings; into what moves you, and why. He brings the wisdom and sensitivity of the Father into the struggles of your life; the disappointments; the unmet expectations; the unspoken, unworded demands. May you lift every thought and care to Him and say once more, "Jesus, I trust in You." May you come to know and believe and trust in the love of your Father.

32

"Whether you turn to the right or to the left, your ears will hear a voice behind you, saying, 'This is the way; walk in it'" (Is 30:21).

"All this also comes from the Lord Almighty, wonderful in counsel and magnificent in wisdom" (Is 28:29).

"I am the Lord your God, who teaches you what is best for you, who directs you in the way you should go" (Is 48:17).

(Col 3:16, Is 43:1, Ps 107:29, Is 49:10, Ro 8:14, Ps 68:5-6, Ps 143:10, Ps 25:5)

He restores your soul

"...the God of all grace...will Himself restore you and make you strong, firm and steadfast" (1 Pe 5:10).

Jesus, the Resurrection and the Life, welcomes you into His Father's family and begins a sensitive work of restoration. Through the power of the Holy Spirit you are being changed, day by day, into His image and likeness. Jesus is your restoration. May you accept the wholeness He offers you today. May Jesus, your Healer, give you a deep desire for wellness in body, mind and spirit. May you entrust the process to Him. May you experience the Life of Jesus in every cell in your body--your mind, emotions, actions and reactions. May He drive away every sickness and disease of body, mind and spirit. He is the Balm of Gilead, the Medicine of your soul.

May you experience His resurrection power that opens prison doors; breaks the chains that bind; casts out demons; multiplies food; calms the storm; walks on water; and brings the dead

33

to life. May you know that nothing is impossible with your loving Heavenly Father. May you trust in His kindness and understanding, that allows growing room; that encourages you to grow and learn and think and feel. May you believe in His compassion, that calls mistakes "opportunities for growth." May you know Him as the God of second chances, and third, and fourth. The Holy Spirit is breathing fresh hope into the deepest and most wounded areas of your life. May the part that hurts the most, say, "Jesus, I trust in You."

As a forgiven child of our Father, may you forgive those who make life hard for you. The forgiveness of Jesus flows from the grace of the cross, through you to those who hurt you. Let it flow. May you recall how Jesus brought people together; to forgive; to reconcile. May that same Spirit be yours. May you risk being open, and sharing your heart.

May you experience deep connection with your Heavenly Father and, through Him, deep connections with brothers and sisters in Christ. Those deep connections will bring healing and stability to your life. May you stay open and connected to family and rooted in a praying community. May all the hurts of your life be healed in the love of Jesus. May you _____.

Jesus, who is Life, is pouring His Life into you now, to be your life. May you come to know and believe and trust in the love of your Father.

♥

"...the God of all grace, who called you to His eternal glory in Christ, after you have suffered a

little while, will Himself restore you and make you strong, firm and steadfast" (1 Pe 5:10).

"...neither death nor life, neither angels nor demons, neither the present or the future, nor any powers, neither height nor depth, nor anything else in all creation, will be able to separate us from the love of God that is in Christ Jesus our Lord" (Ro 8:38-39).

"...I have set before you life and death, blessings and curses. Now choose life, so that you and your children may live and that you may love the Lord your God, listen to His voice, and hold fast to Him. For the Lord is your life..." (Dt 30:19-20).

(Ro 8:11, Dt. 32:10, Jb 11:18, Col 1:27, Ro 8:11, Is 4:8, Mt 6:14, 1 Jn 3:1-2)

He leads you in paths of righteousness for His name's sake

"Blessed be the God and Father of our Lord Jesus Christ, who has blessed us in Christ with every spiritual blessing in the heavenly places, even as He chose us in Him before the foundation of the world, that we should be holy and blameless before Him" (Eph 1:3-4 RSV).

Jesus, Lover of Mankind, takes you into your Father's presence and places you on His lap. God the Father, Abba, Daddy, re-parents you, re-fathers you, and fills that special place in your soul that belongs to Him alone. May His approval and unconditional love infuse you with life-giving energy and a sense of rightness deep inside. As His love permeates your whole being, may you experience your feet being firmly planted on solid rock, in His righteousness.

Jesus, the Font of all Holiness, draws you with cords of love into His sanctified life. May His tender, uncompromising love burn away any residue of unlove or unlovableness in your heart. May Jesus, the Light of your soul, reveal any secret ambitions and deceptions in your heart that would cloud your relationship or divert you from His path of love. May your intimacy with Jesus be so fresh and pure and alive that you automatically turn away from thoughts and ideas that take you away from Him. May your heart become sweet and open, reflecting the beauty of Jesus and the radiance of the Father. May you _____. May you come to know and believe and trust in the love of your Father.

♥

"Create in me a pure heart, O God..." (Ps 51:10).

"...put on the new self, created to be like God in true righteousness and holiness" (Eph 4:24).

"His divine power has given us everything we need for life and godliness through our knowledge of Him who called us by His own glory and goodness. Through these He has given us His very great and precious promises, so that through them you may participate in the divine nature..." (2 Pe 1:3-4).

(Dn 12:3, Pr 3:5, Ps 24:3-4, Eph 4:22-24, Mt 25:34, 1 Th 3:13, Php 1:11, Ps 119:19, Ps 119:11, Ep 5:26, 2 Jn 6, Ps 119:88, Jude 21)

When you walk through the valley of the shadow of death you will fear no evil, for He is with you

"Do not be afraid, for I am with you..." (Is 43:5).

Jesus, the well-lighted path to the Father, walks hand-in-hand with you whenever you go in and out of places of challenge and adversity. May you trust Him as your courage and know Him as your safety. Jesus, your Peace in dark places, reminds you that you can face any challenge without anxiety. May you remember that the peace is there because the relationship is there; may you feel the strength of His love that dispels the fear. As you struggle with temptation to fear, may you reach for His hand and say, "Jesus, I trust in You."

Jesus is your victory. The triumphant right hand of the Lord leads you, the strong arm of the Lord protects you, and the wisdom of the Lord guides you. Jesus makes your feet like the feet of a deer in the valley of opportunity and on your march up victory mountain. May you run and not grow weary, and soar on eagles' wings as you continue your journey with Jesus. May you know Him more intimately and trust Him more completely because of the times with Him in the valley. He is Emmanuel, God with us; and He never goes away. May you _____. May you come to know and believe and trust in the love of your Father.

"For I am the Lord, your God, who takes hold of your right hand and says to you, 'Do not fear; I will help you'" (Is 41:13).

"I have given you authority to trample on snakes and scorpions and to overcome all the power of the enemy; nothing will harm you" (Lk 10:19).

"The sovereign Lord is my strength; He makes my feet like the feet of a deer, He enables me to go on the heights" (Hab 3:19).

(Ro 8:37, Is 41:10, Is 42:16, Is 40:31, Col 1:2, 1 Jn 4:18, 2 Co 12:9, Ps 91:9-15, 2 Th 2:16-17)

His rod and staff will comfort you

"...I am He who comforts you..." (Is 51:12).

Jesus, your Advocate, is here to be what you need. All you have to do is ask. May you know His readiness to help; His desire to comfort and protect; His ability to guide; His power to heal. May you experience His intimate identification with you; His feeling your feelings; His crying your tears. Jesus, your Champion and Shield, invites you to hear Him, trust Him, and receive His life.

Jesus, your Protection and Guide, is both your safety and the one who pushes you out of the nest in due season. May you trust Him when He takes you beyond your comfort zone. May your trust in Jesus enable you to test your wings and venture out to new horizons. He invites you to ask for more; to be stretched; to allow Him to prepare you for opportunities and adventures that lie ahead. May the rod and the staff of your Shepherd, set you apart and equip you for a work of loving service.

As Peter's mother-in-law was healed and then she served, may your time in the nesting place, in the healing presence of the Shepherd, prepare you for a life of service. May your eyes be opened and your heart awakened to the needs of others. May you begin to reach out to them with His love. May their eyes be opened to the love of God, because of your healing touch. May you _____. May you both come to know and believe and trust in the love of your Father.

"The Lord will keep you from all harm--He will watch over your life; the Lord will watch over your coming and going both now and evermore" (Ps 121:7-8).

"The Lord delights in the way of the man whose steps He has made firm; though he stumble, he will not fall, for the Lord upholds him with His hand" (Ps 37:23-24).

"Praise be to the God and Father of our Lord Jesus Christ, the Father of compassion and the God of all comfort, who comforts us in all our troubles, so that we can comfort those in any trouble with the comfort we ourselves have received from God" (2 Cor 1:3-4).

(Ps 91:2, Ps 103:13, Jn 17:11, Ps 115:15, 1 Co 1:3, Ge 28:15, Ps 121:4, Jn 17:11, 2 Ti 1:12)

He prepares a table for you in the presence of your enemies

"He has taken me to the banquet hall, and His banner over me is love" (SS 2:4).

Jesus, your Victory, seats you at His banquet of love where all your enemies can see you. May you feast under His banner of love in the company of those who are not your friends. May you recognize His provision in these circumstances.

May you realize that you can relax and enjoy yourself wherever you are, because God is in charge. May you remember that no weapon formed against you can prosper. Jesus is your armor. His belt of truth protects you from lies. His breastplate of righteousness protects you from sin. His shoes of peace protect you through forgiveness. His helmet of salvation reminds you of who you are in Him. His shield of faith reminds you that He is in charge. His sword of the Spirit is His living Word of protection. Praying in the Spirit protects you through ongoing intimate communion.

May He show you the times He has helped you; carried you; stood beside you; intervened on your behalf. He has been your safe path through the sea of difficulties; your fresh water in the desert; your protection from the snare of evil. He has turned curses into blessings and brought good out of situations that could have left you defeated.

Through the table He has prepared in the presence of unfriendly company, may you see and remember how His powerful hand has delivered you in the past. He is the Wall of Fire around you, the Mighty One of Israel. Praise His holy name.

May your heart fill with gratitude for all He has done. May you _____.
May you come to know and believe and trust in the love of your Father.

"They feast on the abundance of Your house; You give them drink from Your river of delights" (Ps 36:8).

"For you did not receive a spirit that makes you a slave again to fear, but you received the Spirit of sonship. And by Him we cry, 'Abba, Father.' The Spirit Himself testifies with our spirit that we are God's children. Now if we are children, then we are heirs--heirs of God and coheirs with Christ, if indeed we share in His sufferings in order that we may also share in His glory" (Ro 8:15-17).

"From the fullness of His grace we have all received one blessing after another" (Jn 1:16).

(Is 55:12, Is 55:1, Jn 6:51, Pr 17:7, Ps 31:19, Dt 1:29-31, 2 Th 2:16-17, Ps 92:11, Ep 6:12-17)

He anoints your head with oil

"...you will receive power when the Holy Spirit comes on you; and you will be My witnesses...to the ends of the earth" (Ac 1:8).

Jesus, the Anointed One, sent forth by our Father, blesses you with the oil of His Spirit. He consecrates you to His service and dedicates you to His purposes. He is the love and power in your life. May His anointing release you for service to others. May you experience Him as your empowerment, to go where your Father sends you and do what He wants you to do.

May He anoint your mind, that it be receptive to the wisdom of the Spirit, and discerning of things not from the Spirit. May you have the mind of Christ, think His thoughts, understand

41

and cooperate with His nature and purposes. May He anoint your eyes, that they burn with the fire of His love, with a vision that is deep and high and wide and centered on His purposes. May He anoint your ears, that you would hear with hope and compassion and forgiveness. May He anoint your mouth, that it would speak words of life and truth to set people free. May He anoint your hands, that they communicate His love and His power; bringing His healing, freeing touch. May He anoint your feet, that they would walk in obedience born of love, and carry His good news to a hurting world.

May you live today and every day in the nature of Jesus Christ, bowed down in worship before your Father, and filled with holy power. May you recognize the fiery zeal of Christ and make room for that same passion in your life. May the Holy Spirit light a deep fire in your heart.

The oil of the Spirit, a strong, holy current flowing in your life, is lifting you to new horizons of service. May you continue to walk in the anointing of the Spirit day by day. May you _____. May you come to know and believe and trust in the love of your Father.

♥

"...He will baptize you with the Holy Spirit and with fire" (Mt 3:11).

"...His word is in my heart like a burning fire, shut up in my bones. I am weary of holding it in; indeed, I cannot" (Jer 20:89).

"...be filled with the Spirit" (Ep 5:18).

(Zech 4:6, 1 Th 2:4, 1 Ti 1:14, Jn 1:16, Ac 13:52, 2 Ti 1:6, Mic 3:8, 2 Co 3:6, 1 Ti 1:12)

Your cup overflows

"...Freely you have received, freely give" (Mt 10:8).

Jesus, the free gift of the Father, overflows in your life like streams in the desert. May you feel His resurrection life pouring through you, bringing healing and deliverance to others. May you experience the generosity of Jesus and receive this same virtue. May your heart be so overflowing with love for your Heavenly Father, because of all He has done for you, that you just want to do whatever He wants. May He increase your capacity to receive others in love. May your ears be sensitive to His call for workers in His harvest. May you hear His personal call, and say in response, "Here I am, send me." May your trust in Him continue to grow.

May He pour His life through you extravagantly, with blessings that bring healing and restoration. Jesus, who brings you the blessing of our Father, extends favor to others through you. May you testify to what He has done for you, and tell of His works with joy. May your life be a witness to the power of God. Jesus, our Hope, brings great hope to others through you. Jesus, our Healer, heals others through you. Jesus, the Fountain of Living Water, pours His life into others through you. Jesus, the Bread of Life, feeds others through you. Jesus, your Freedom, sets others free through you. Jesus, your Victory, brings others to victory through you. Our God is an awesome God. Praise His holy name.

Knowing who you are in Him, may you take up your tambourines and engage life with a spirit of adventure, with holy wonder, with the wide eyes of a child. May you have the courage to recognize and follow your dreams. May you _____. May you come to know and believe and trust in the love of your Father.

♥

"Then I heard the voice of the Lord saying, 'Whom shall I send? And who will go for us?' And I said, 'Here am I. Send me'" (Is 6:8).

"...let your light shine before men, that they may see your good deeds and praise your Father in heaven" (Mt 5:16).

"...Go into all the world and preach the good news to all creation" (Mk 16:15).

(Ps 66:16, Mt 25:35-36, Jer 31:4, 1 Pe 2:9, 2 Co 1:5, Ps 119:171, Ro 15:13, Jn 4:35, Mt 9:37, Lk 10:2, 2 Co 4:15, Ep 6:19, Ro 9:17)

Surely goodness and mercy will follow you all the days of your life

"...I chose you to go and bear fruit--fruit that will last. Then the Father will give you whatever you ask in My name. This is My command: Love each other" (Jn 15:16-17).

Jesus, the goodness and mercy of our Father, blesses you with a fruitful life, lived in the power of the Holy Spirit. May goodness and mercy continually accompany you, as you daily walk with Jesus--making up for any lack, preventing or bringing good out of difficult situations. May you know that this favor is yours, as a child of the King. May you be awakened to the knowledge that you are living your life in His merciful love.

Knowing this, may you experience freedom to sing and cry and laugh and dream. May you enjoy yourself as you are, and others as they are. May you so deeply know and believe and trust in the love of your Father that you can enjoy other people's talents and gifts as much as your own. May you be enriched by the differences of others, because you are so rooted in love and secure in your own identity in Christ.

The fruit of the Spirit continues to grow in your life. Jesus, by His Spirit, produces in your life an abundance of peace, love and joy, goodness and mercy, kindness and patience, gentleness and self-control. May everything you do prosper; may you long enjoy the work of your hands. May you _____. May you come to know and believe and trust in the love and the goodness and mercy of your Father.

"He is like a tree planted by streams of water, which yields its fruit in season and whose leaf does not wither. Whatever he does prospers" (Ps 1:3).

"This is to My Father's glory, that you bear much fruit, showing yourselves to be My disciples" (Jn 15:8).

"And we, who with unveiled faces all reflect the Lord's glory, are being transformed into His likeness with ever-increasing glory, which comes from the Lord, who is the Spirit" (2 Cor 3:18).

(Jas 3:17, Gal 5:22-23, Is 65:22, Ro 10:15, Heb 4:15, 2 Ti 1:6, Is 63:9, Ps 33:5, Ro 1:7, Jas 1:17-18)

"I am the vine; you are the branches. If a man remains in Me and I in him, he will bear much fruit..." (Jn 15:5).

Jesus, the Savior of the World, has enabled you to recognize your need for Him. By His grace you have said, "Jesus, I trust in You," and surrendered your life into His care. You know you are safe in Him. May you remember with love all He has done for you. May you recognize that you are learning to see life and circumstances through His eyes of love. You are continually being touched and restored by the power of the Holy Spirit. May you see that every act of service to your brothers and sisters is an act of worship of your Heavenly Father. May you know that your praise is a blessing to your Heavenly Father; that you "bless the Lord" with your praise.

May you realize that you are becoming a person of deep prayer, knowing that the strength and freedom of your life comes from communion with your Father, the Everlasting One, your Reality. May you always treasure and protect and nurture that communion. May it be a number one priority in your life. May you know His pleasure in your response to His love. May you truly know the healing power of your Father's blessing. May you _____.

Jesus, the Name above all names, son of the King Immortal, takes you with Him to the Jordan River, and opens your ears to listen deeply to the covenant words of your Father: *"You are My child, whom I love; with you I am well pleased"* (Lk 3:21). May those words be permanently engraved on your heart. In life and in death, throughout time and into eternity, may you forever say, "Jesus, I trust in You." May you know and believe and trust in the love of your Father. Amen.

"Come, let us bow down in worship, let us kneel before the Lord our Maker; for He is our God and we are the people of His pasture, the flock under His care" (Ps 95:6-7).

"...Praise and glory and wisdom and thanks and honor and power and strength be to our God forever and ever..." (Rev 7:12).

"Now to the King eternal, immortal, invisible, the only God, be honor and glory for ever and ever" (1 Ti 1:17).

(Ps 126:3, Ps 69:9, Jn 2:17, Ro 12:11, Ps 149:1, 1 Jn 4:16, Ps 103:1, Is 46:4, Mt 6:6, Ps 21:6, Gal 6:8, 1 Jn 5:11)

"Our Father, who art in heaven, hallowed be Your name. Your kingdom come. Your will be done, on earth, as it is in heaven. Give us this day our daily bread, and forgive us our trespasses, as we forgive those who trespass against us. And lead us not into temptation, but deliver us from evil. For Thine is the kingdom and the power and the glory for ever and ever. Amen."

IV

Suggestions for Use

The Father's Blessing can be given by a father to his children. It can be prayed by a stand-in, or spiritual father one-on-one or in groups. It can be read and received directly in prayer by anyone needing a father's blessing. The user is encouraged to adapt it to specific needs.

1. **Father can pray blessing onto audio or videotape:** After praying the blessing onto a tape, a father can make it available to children and grandchildren. It could be played softly when children go to sleep at night, or when a family member is ill, as a strengthening presence.

2. **Prayed by a father with young children:** One portion of the Father's Blessing could be used each day during prayer time with children, after a brief discussion of the meaning of the particular topic. Young children could draw pictures of their idea of a blessing, and describe how they feel about the blessing. The prayer can be used as an opportunity to help young children get in touch with the love of their Heavenly Father. The words in the blessing can be simplified to match the age group.

3. **Fathers with adult children:** The father can use it as an opportunity to ask forgiveness for any lack of blessing in earlier years. Adult children could use the opportunity to express to their father any "implied" blessings they received from him. There might be a time of prayer and forgiveness for healing of negative experiences. (When I was with my adult nieces and nephews at their father's funeral, I asked each of them to share a blessing received from their father. Linda Sue said, "He gave me wide eyes, a broad perspective in life." Todd said, "He gave me a sense of creativity and allowed me to make my own mistakes." Darren said, "He gave me a gift of compassion and spiritual heritage." Lori said, "He gave me a sense of fun and a sense of responsibility." These were all "implied" blessings. How much better if we can share them with fathers before they die!)

4. **Prayer by a stand-in father with groups:** The stand-in father could begin by sharing his own experience of fathers who helped him along the way, and how God provides substitute fathers. He could lay hands on each one and pray individual blessings. Depending on group size, they might form small groups and share personal experiences of blessing.

5. **Prayer by a stand-in father one-on-one:** As an introduction to the blessing, he might represent a natural father and ask forgiveness for hurts and abuses received. For example: "On behalf of your father, I ask forgiveness for all the ways you were hurt as a child. I ask the Lord to make it up to you for all injuries received."

6. **Prayed individually:** In a comfortable place of prayer you might pray the blessing, asking the Lord to give you the experience of a Father's blessing in your heart. Or you might play the tape of the Father's Blessing (see order form).

7. **In fatherless homes:** A male relative could pray the blessing for the children. Or, the mother could pray it as from God the Father. As another alternative, the tape of the Father Blessing could be played. Close with laying hands on the sons and daughters and giving them an individual blessing.

8. **Clergy use:** Male clergy can be representative fathers praying the blessing. Catholic priests or clergy from churches offering the sacrament of reconciliation can incorporate this sacrament in the healing process.

9. **Prayer groups:** One possibility is a thirteen week program, focussing each week on a different section of the Father's Blessing.

"May God Himself, the God of peace, sanctify you through and through. May your whole spirit, soul and body be kept blameless at the coming of our Lord Jesus Christ. The one who calls you is faithful and He will do it" (1 Th 5:23-24).

Father Blessing Order Form

$3.00 Each
Quantity Discount Available

Quantity _____

Total price _____

Plus shipping _____

California residents add 8% sales tax _____

(Calculate Shipping From *Miracle Hour* Chart on Next Page)

Total enclosed _____

Ship to _____

_____

_____

Phone _____

Send check or money order payable to Miracles of the Heart Ministries, P.O. Box 4034, Santa Clara, CA 95056. To order from outside the U.S., please send $5.00 per book ($3.00 for book and $2.00 for shipping) in U.S. FUNDS ONLY to above address. Write for quantity discount. For questions, telephone or fax (408) 734-8663.

Miracle Hour — $2.00 — A simple format for a daily hour of prayer. This simple book provides the structure for prayer to help direct your time and attention. Includes suggestions for specific prayer of praise, intercession, surrender, etc. English and Spanish.

Miracle Hour Order Form

Quantity Prices for U.S. Orders		Add Shipping
1-5 Copies	$2.00 ea.	$2.00
6-25 Copies	2.00 ea.	3.00
26-50 Copies	1.75 ea.	4.00
51-99 Copies	1.50 ea.	5.00
100 + Copies	1.35 ea.	6.00 per 100
* Bookstores Write for Discount		

Quantity: English _____ Spanish _____

Total Price _____

Plus Shipping _____

California Residents Add 8% Sales Tax _____

Total Enclosed █████████████

Ship to _____

_____

_____

Phone _____

Send check or money order payable to Miracles of the Heart Ministries, P.O. Box 4034, Santa Clara, CA 95056. To order from outside the U.S., please send $4.00 ($2.00 for book and $2.00 for shipping) in U.S. funds to the above address. Write for quantity discount. For questions, telephone or fax (408) 734-8663.

VIDEO SERIES

We now have four broadcast-quality videotapes (ten 26-minute segments, or five hours of viewing) formatted for public access television stations, as follows:

Tape 1 — Side 1 — Linda's testimony
              Side 2 — Forgiveness...steps to victory   1 Hour

Tape 2 — Four segments on book, the "Miracle Hour...a method of prayer that will change your life"   2 Hours

Tape 3 — Two segments on book, "Five-Minute Miracles...praying for people with simplicity and power"   1 Hour

Tape 4 — Two segments on book, "The Healing Power of a Father's Blessing"   1 Hour

Send form and check or money order in U.S. funds to Linda Schubert, Miracles of the Heart Ministries, P.O. Box 4034, Santa Clara, CA 95056, phone/fax (408) 734-8663. One-hour videos are $15.00 each. Two-hour video is $20.00.

Please send: Tape 1_____ Tape 2_____

Tape 3_____ Tape 4_____ Total $_____

Complete set $65.00_____

California residents add 8% sales tax_____

Shipping $_____

Total enclosed $_____

Shipping to U.S. locations
1 tape $2.00   2-3 tapes $2.50   4 tapes $3.00

Ship to_____

_____

_____

Phone_____

CASSETTE TAPE ORDER FORM
$4.00 Each

Quantity

_____ Miracle Hour Prayers (for those who want just the prayers on cassette)

_____ Miracle Hour Workshop (teaching and practice sessions)

_____ Giving Thanks (the healing power of a grateful heart)

_____ Forgiveness (steps to victory)

_____ Simple one-on-one prayer ministry (teaching and practical steps in praying with people)

_____ Linda's personal testimony

The Healing Power of a Father's Blessing

_____ Tape 1 — The Teaching

_____ Tape 2 — The Prayer of Blessing

Tapes $4.00 each. Total enclosed $_____.Add $2.00 shipping 1-5 tapes and 10% of total for more than 5. California residents add 8% sales tax.

SCRIPTURE FOCUS TAPE SERIES

In this gentle but powerful series, Linda begins with a definition of the topic (strength, trust, etc.), then reads scriptures on the theme. The tape ends with a prayer for the Lord to deepen in the listener the experience of strength, trust, etc. The series evolved from the popularity of the "strength" scripture tape. We pray the Holy Spirit will use them to take you deeper into the liberating power of the Word of God.

_____	strength	_____	worship
_____	trust	_____	hope
_____	peace	_____	joy
_____	prayer	_____	wisdom
_____	healing	_____	mercy

Tapes $4.00 each. Total enclosed $_____. (Add $2.00 shipping for 1-5 tapes and 10% of total for more than 5. California residents add 8% sales tax.)

Ship to_____

_____

_____

Phone _____

If you are interested in having Linda come to your area for conferences or workshops, write or phone:
Linda Schubert
Miracles of the Heart Ministries
P.O. Box 4034, Santa Clara, CA 95056

Phone/fax (408) 734-8663